THE FOOTBALL

COLOURING BOOK

Buster Books

ILLUSTRATED BY
CLIVE GOODYER

EDITED BY
JONNY MARX

DESIGNED BY
JACK CLUCAS

First published in Great Britain in 2015 by
Buster Books, an imprint of Michael O'Mara Books Limited,
9 Lion Yard, Tremadoc Road, London SW4 7NQ

W www.busterbooks.co.uk F Buster Children's Books @BusterBooks

Copyright © Buster Books 2015

All rights reserved. No part of this publication may be reproduced, stored in a retrieval
system, or transmitted in any form or by any means, electronic, mechanical, photocopying,
recording or otherwise, without prior permission of the publisher.

A CIP catalogue record for this book is available from the British Library.

ISBN: 978-1-78055-305-4

2 4 6 8 10 9 7 5 3 1

This book was printed in April 2015 by
Shenzhen Wing King Tong Paper Products Co. Ltd., Shenzhen, Guangdong, China.

Papers used by Buster Books are natural, recyclable products made
from wood grown in sustainable forests. The manufacturing processes
conform to the environmental regulations of the country of origin.

TV

The kids are
playing football
in the park.

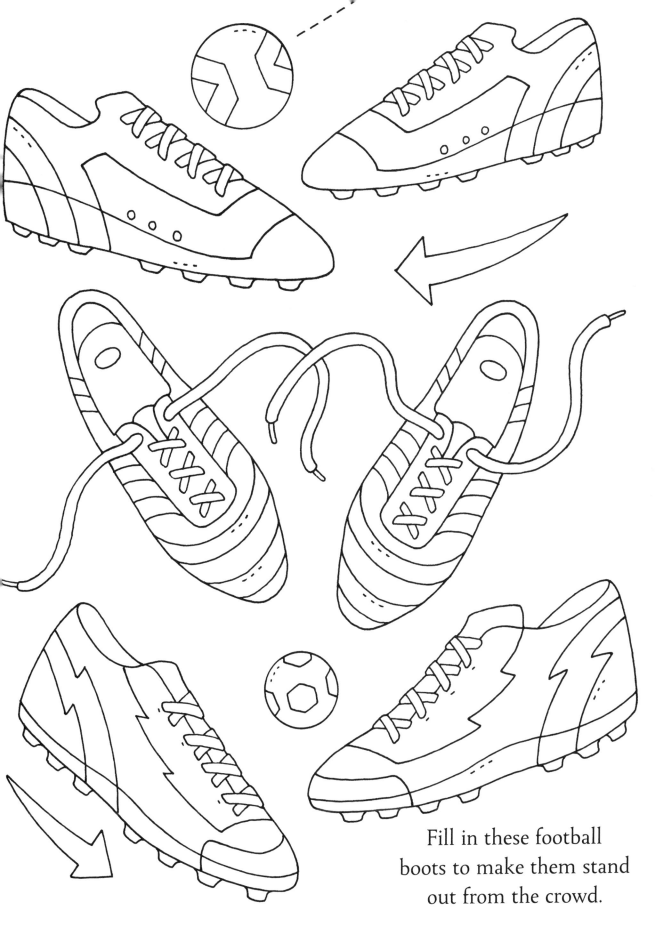

Fill in these football
boots to make them stand
out from the crowd.

The away fans are on the road.

UNITED!

Colour in all
of this football
equipment.

Colour in the trophy-winning squad.

Wow! These football freestylers
are practising their tricks.

RECORD-BREAKING SIGNING!

These match-day tickets
need colouring in.

ASIA XI

EURO XI

KICKOFF – 17.00

SEAT 11, ROW C

RD ROVERS

S

F.C.

The Unbeaten United
VS
Champions X1

Seat 39, Row D
Kickoff – 16.00

WORLD CUP
FINAL

SEAT 122   ROW X

STER BRIGADE
VS
O'MARA F.C.

SOUTH STAND
KICKOFF – 19.30

The players are getting
ready for a big game.

The players are singing the national anthem as loud as they can.

Fill in these
funky footballs
with bright
colours.

It's a free kick. Will she score?

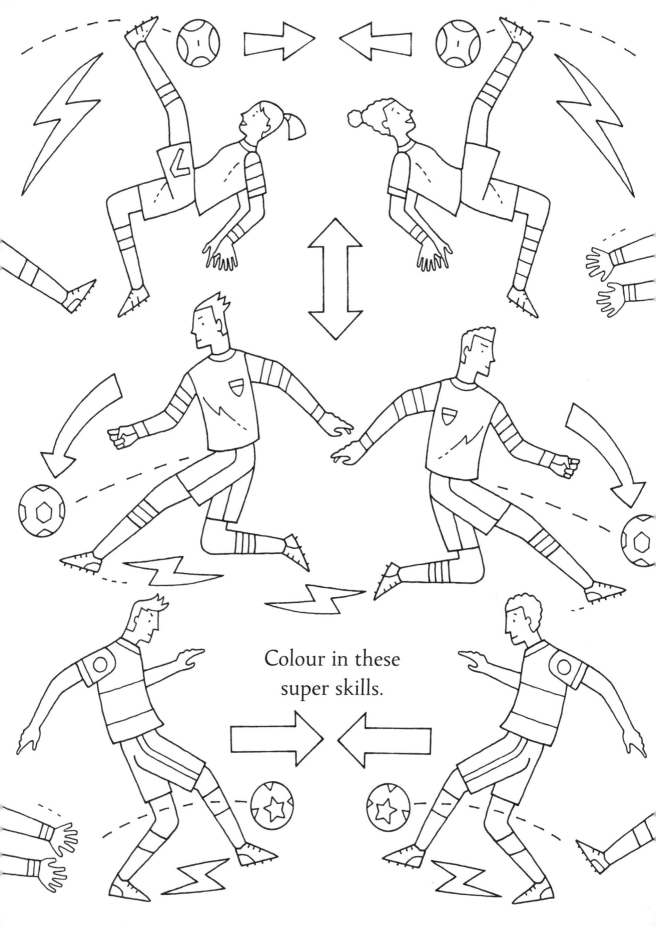

Colour in these
super skills.

Oh no!
It's a red card.

These team shirts need shading in.

These children
are playing football
in the street.

That goal takes her team into the lead.

Fill in these goalkeeper
gloves and water bottles.

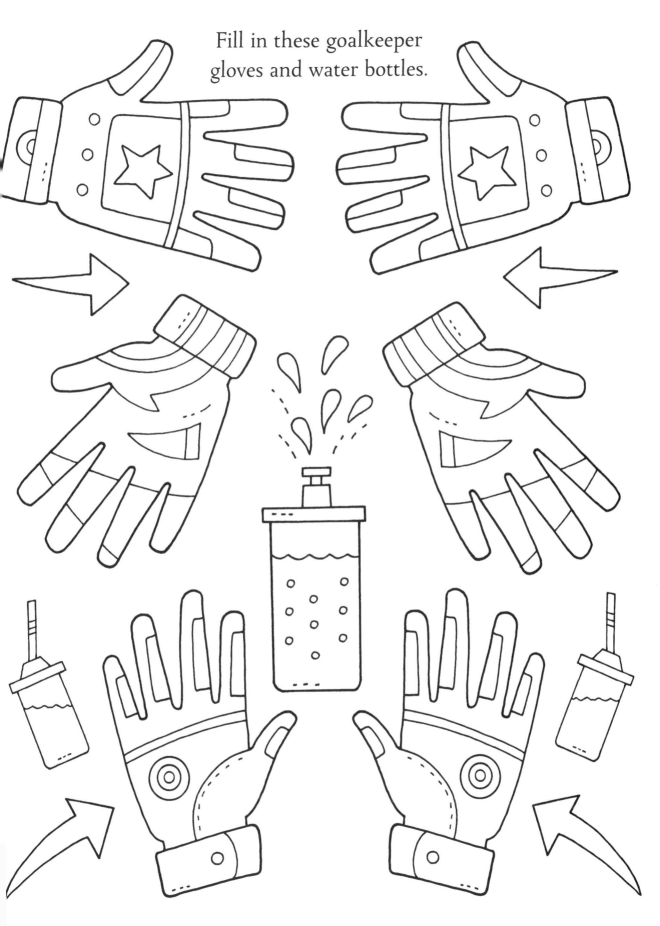

Playing ball
on the beach.

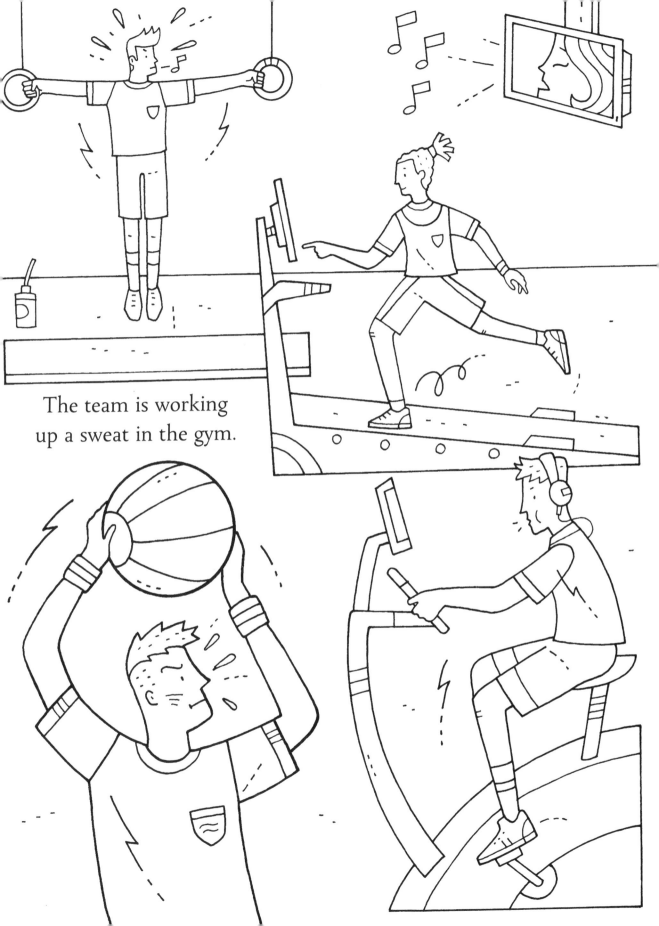

The team is working
up a sweat in the gym.

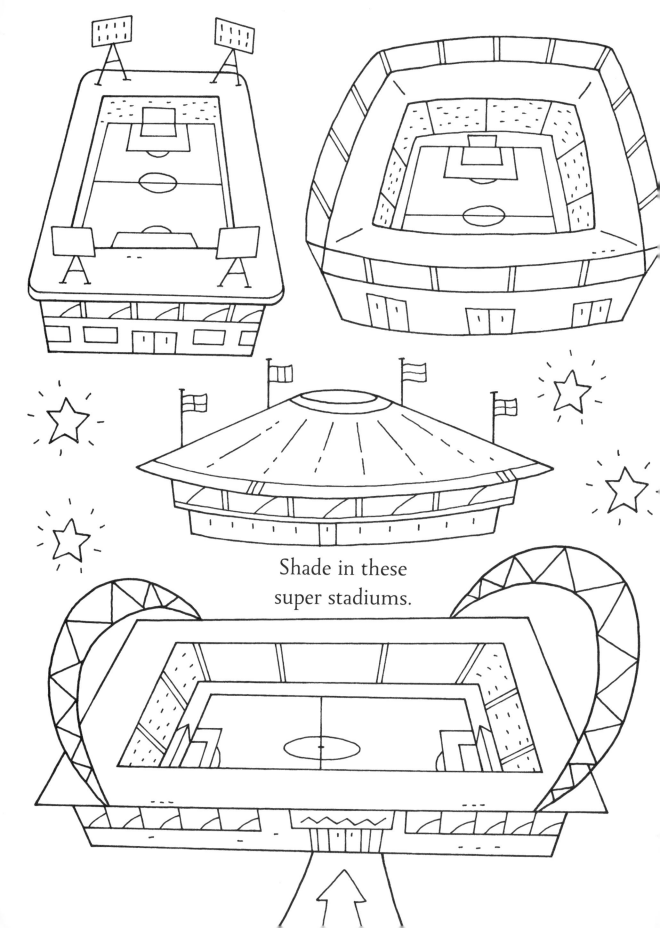

Shade in these
super stadiums.

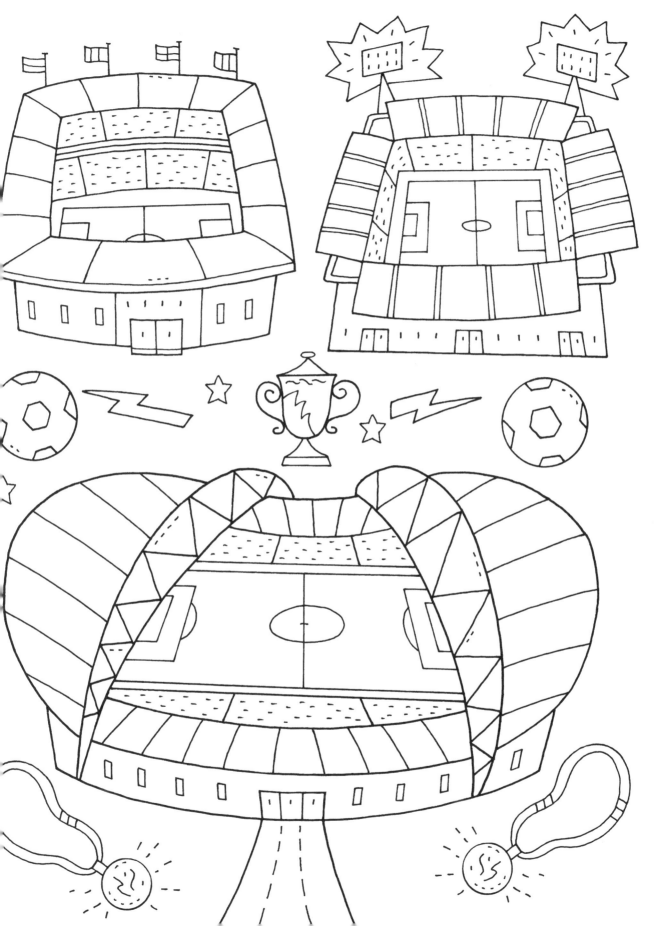

Look at all the trophies and medals.

Shade in the ultimate football boots.

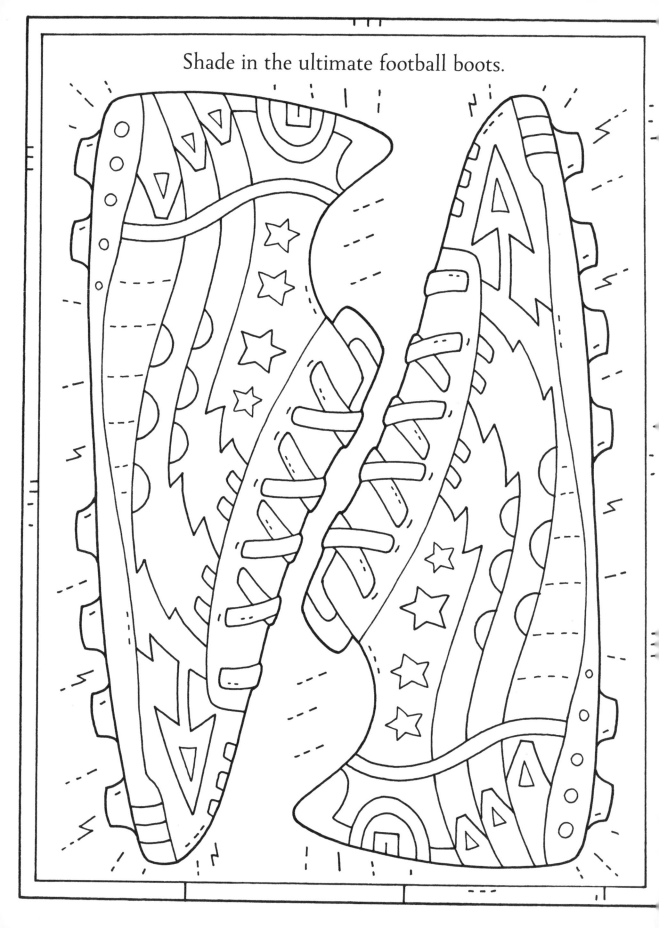

It's time to celebrate.

Even the snowmen
are joining in!

The cup-winning squad
has returned home.

The victorious team is being cheered by the noisy crowd.

1977

Slick McGee

George Better

1902

HALL OF FAME

1925

Dantè The Destroyer

2009

The Raider

1986